MW00983617

THIS COLORING BOOK
BELONGS TO:

______________________________

______________________________

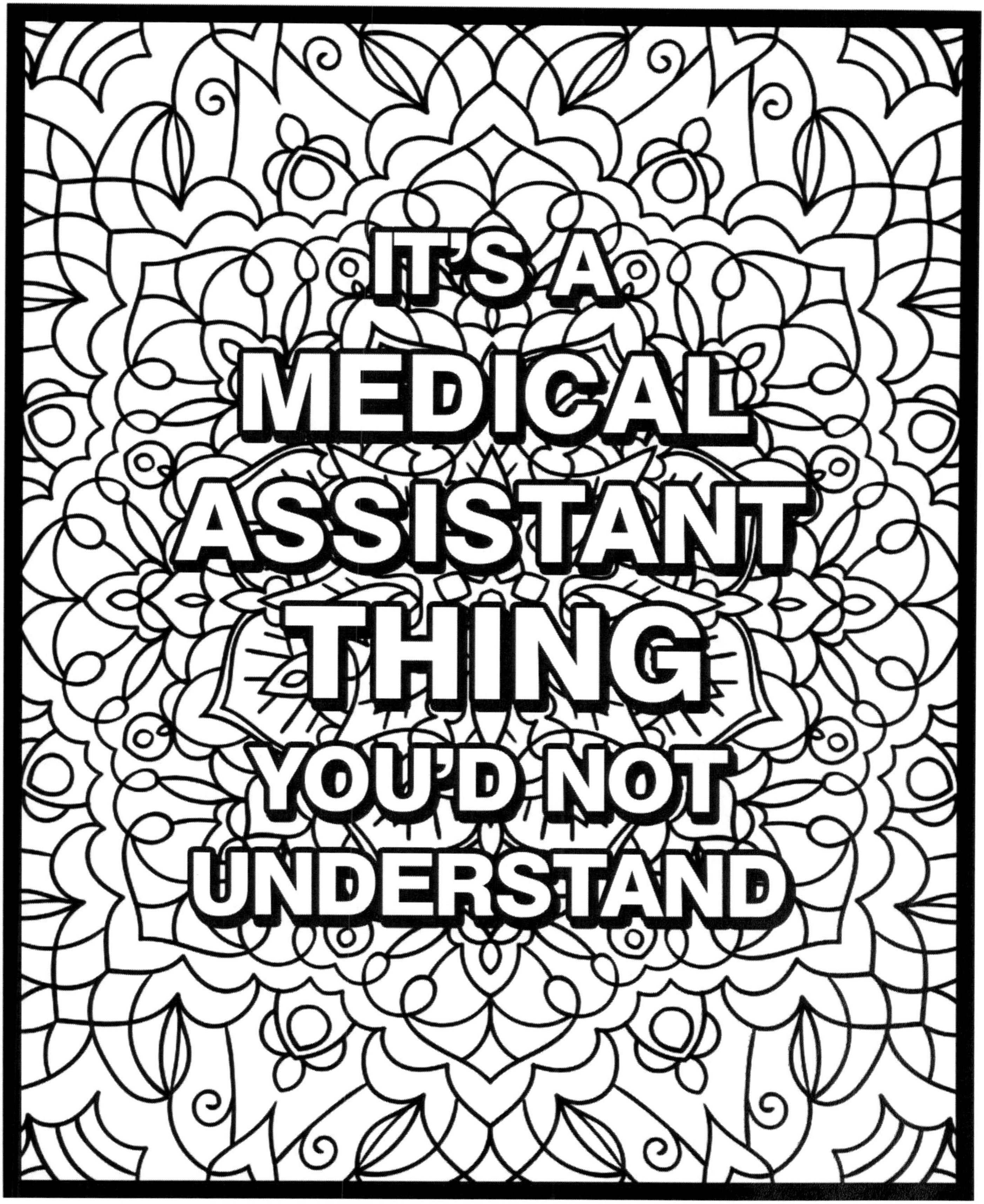
IT'S A
MEDICAL
ASSISTANT
THING
YOU'D NOT
UNDERSTAND

I'VE 99
PROBLEMS
BUT
COLORING
AIN'T ONE

instant
Medical
assistant
Just add
Coffee

STFU!
JUST ASSUME
I'M ALWAYS
RIGHT

JUST A
MEDICAL
ASSISTANT
WHO
SOLEMNLY
SWEARS

I GOT A
GOOD
HEART
but
MY MOUTH

SORRY!
the Nice
MEDICAL
ASSISTANT
IS ON
Vacation

Essential
AF!

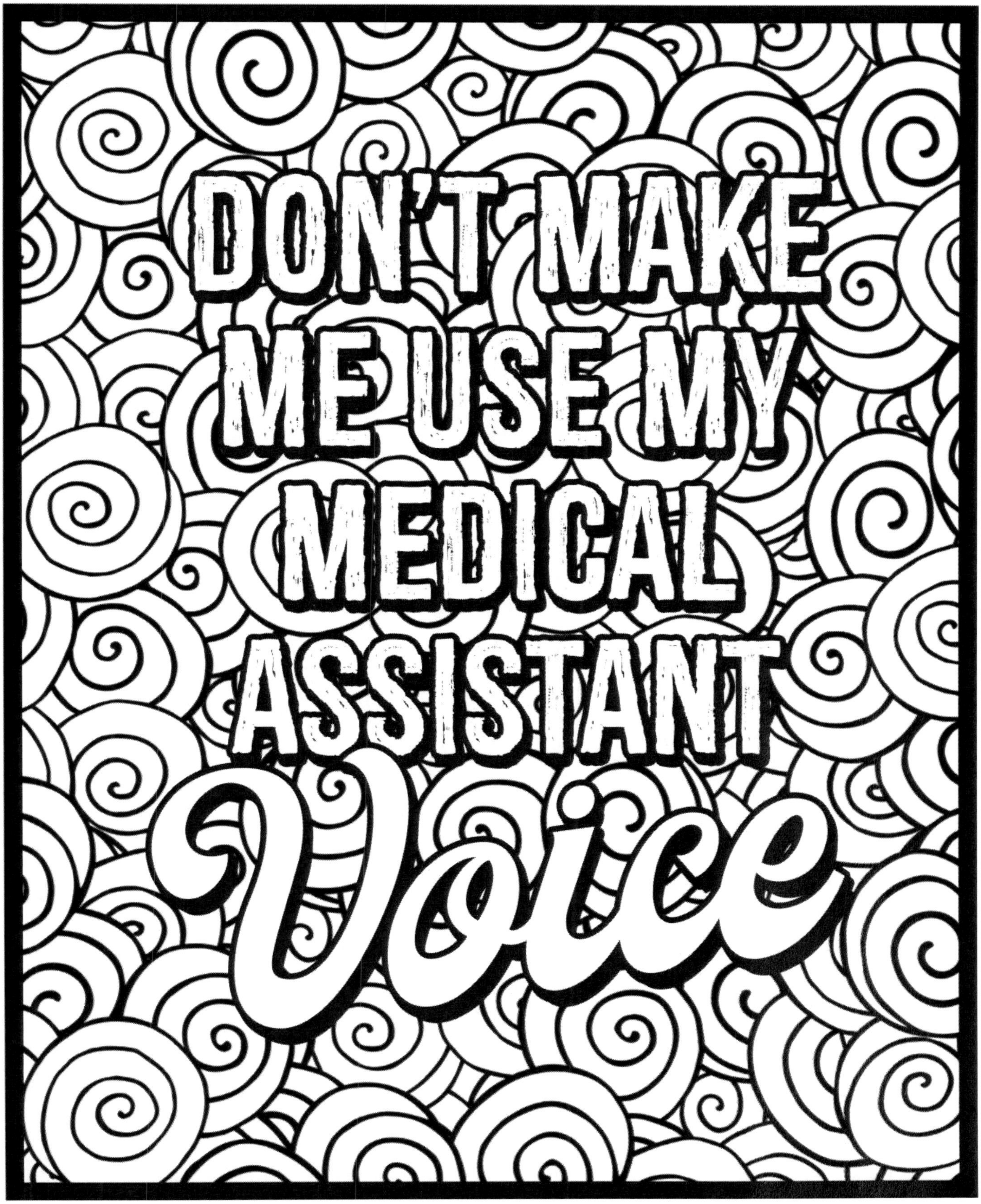
DON'T MAKE
ME USE MY
MEDICAL
ASSISTANT
Voice

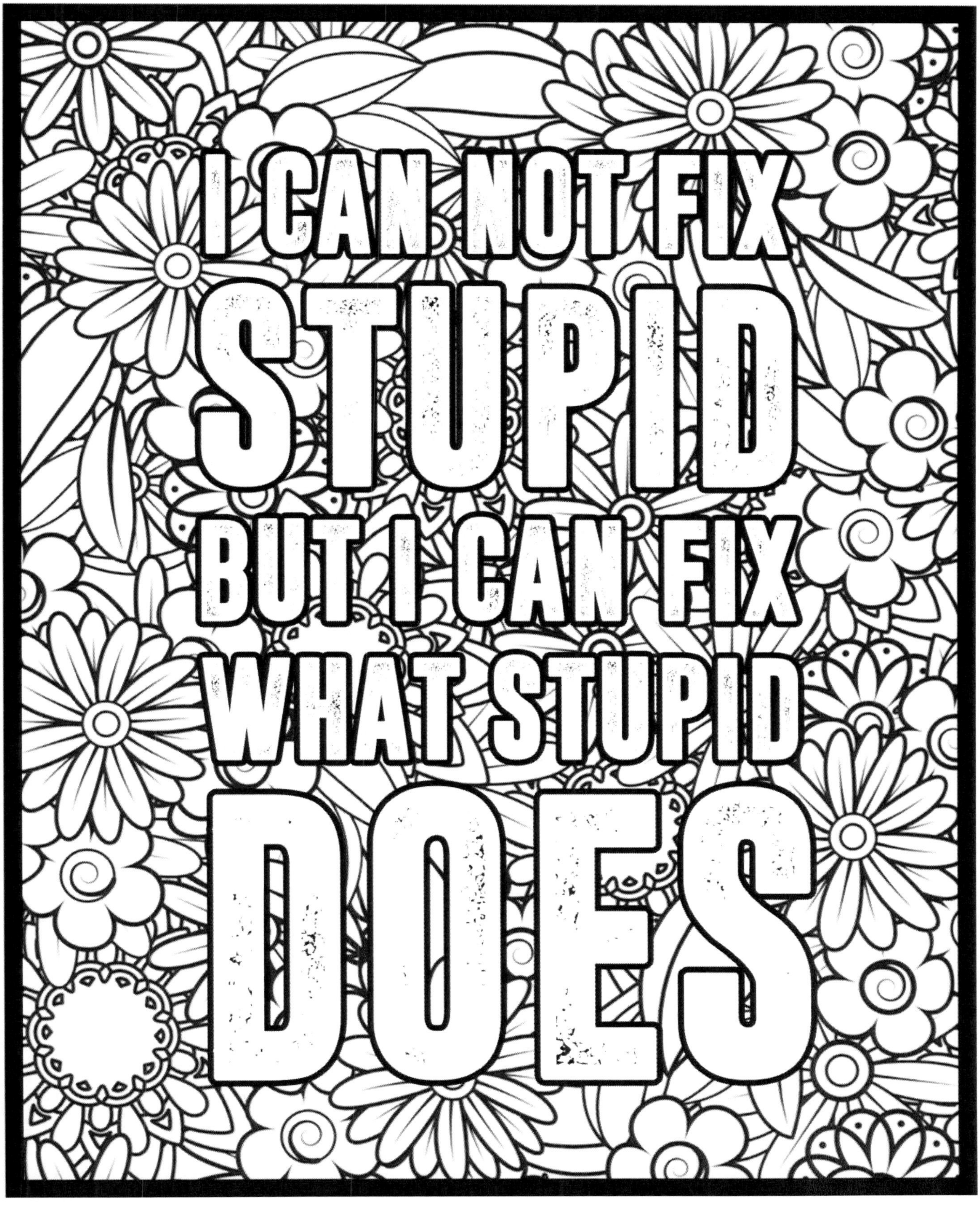
I CAN NOT FIX
STUPID
BUT I CAN FIX
WHAT STUPID
DOES

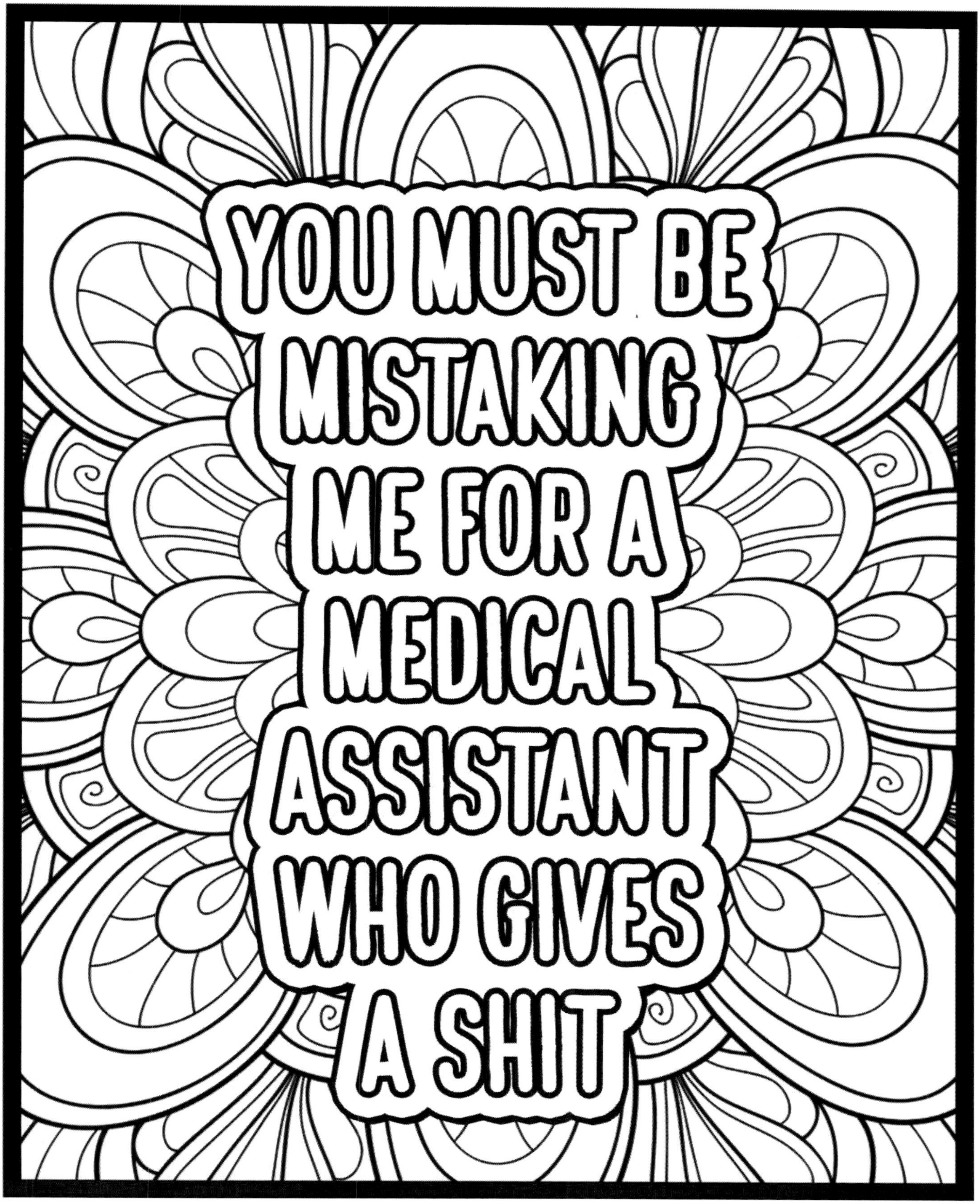
YOU MUST BE
MISTAKING
ME FOR A
MEDICAL
ASSISTANT
WHO GIVES
A SHIT

Of Course
I Talk to
myself
sometimes
i need expert
Advice!

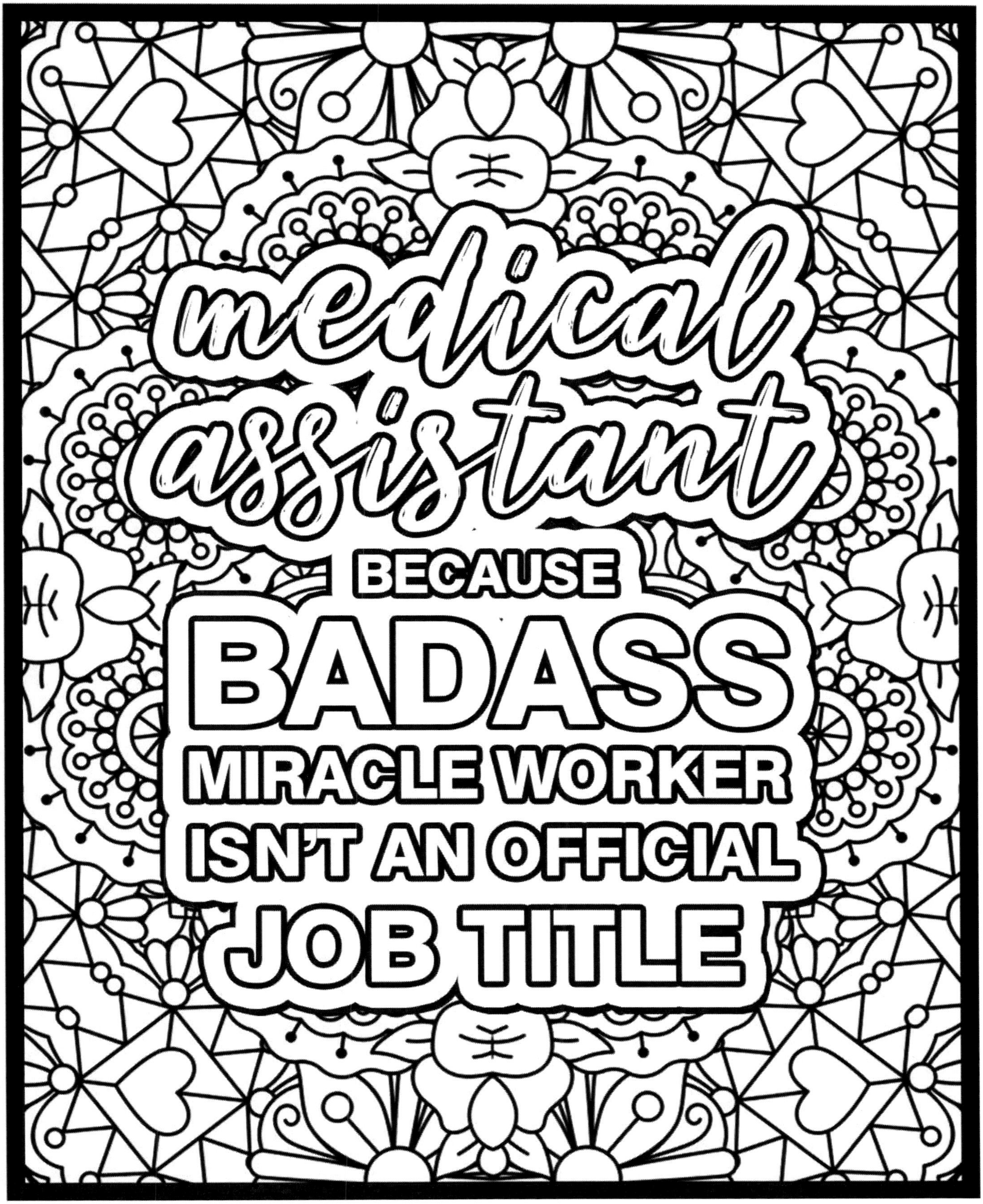
medical assistant
BECAUSE
BADASS
MIRACLE WORKER
ISN'T AN OFFICIAL
JOB TITLE

WORK?!
I ONLY
NEED MY
PAYCHECKS

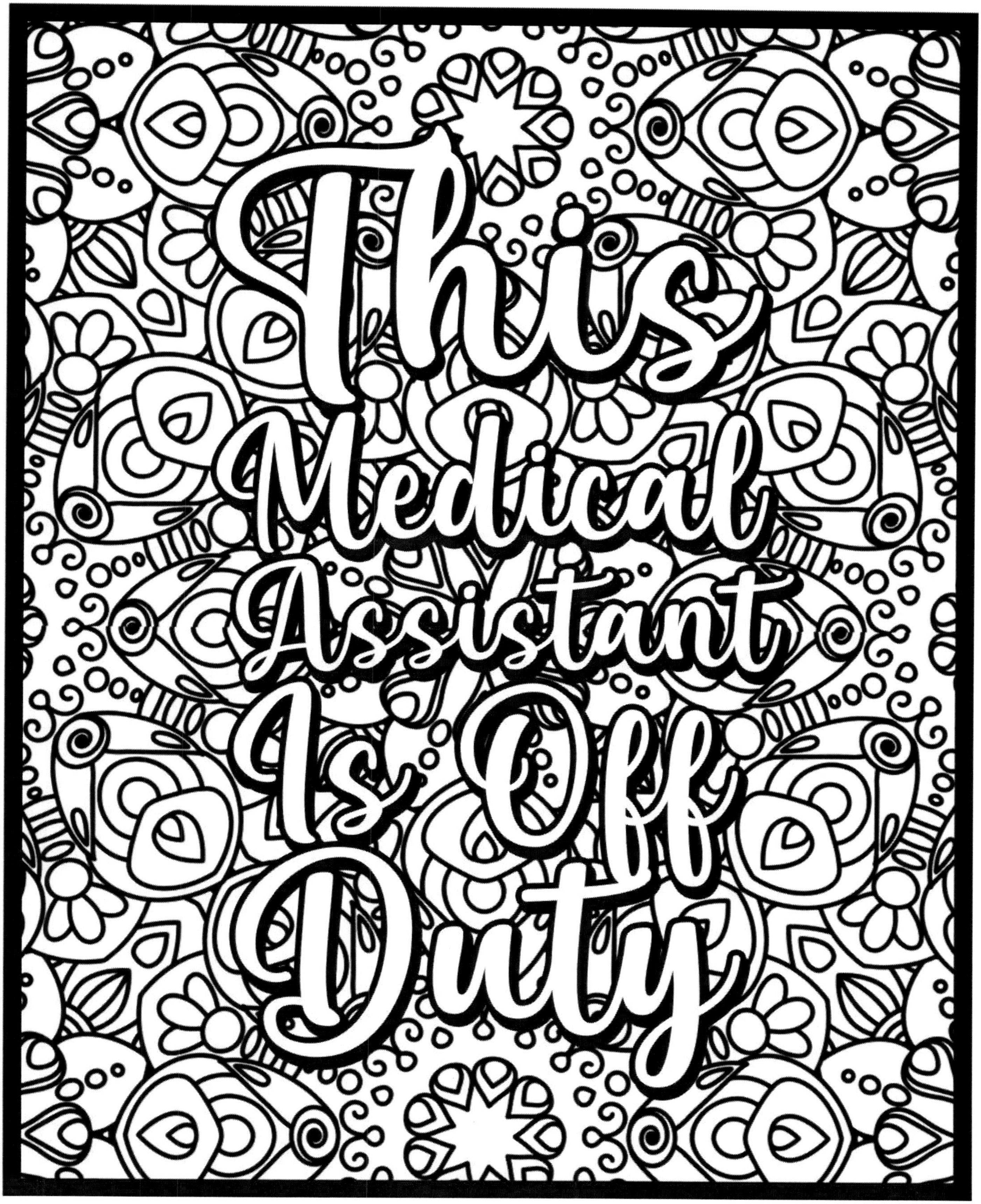
This
Medical
Assistant
Is Off
Duty

CAUTION!
MOOD
SWING
IN PROGRESS

I'm a
MEDICAL
ASSISTANT
WHAT'S
YOUR
SUPER
POWER?

SOME PEOPLE
JUST NEED A
HIGH-FIVE
"IN THE FACE"

SORRY!
I'M DONE
HELPING
ASSHOLES
TODAY

I need a
NAP
& a glass of
wine

Made in United States
North Haven, CT
12 October 2023

42656451R00026